FIRST GRAPHICS

SEASONS

FALL IS FUN

BY CARI MEISTER

ILLUSTRATED BY
JIM LINGENFELTER

CAPSTONE PRESS
a capstone imprint

First Graphics are published by Capstone Press,
151 Good Counsel Drive, P.O. Box 669, Mankato, Minnesota 56002.
www.capstonepub.com

Printed in the United States of America in Stevens Point, Wisconsin.

032010
005741WZF10

Books published by Capstone Press are manufactured with paper containing at least 10 percent post-consumer waste.

Library of Congress Cataloging-in-Publication Data
Meister, Cari.
Fall is fun / by Cari Meister ; illustrated by Jim Lingenfelter.
p. cm.
ISBN 978-1-4296-4731-1 (library binding)
ISBN 978-1-4296-5623-8 (paperback)
1. Autumn—Juvenile literature. I. Title.

QB637.7.M45 2011
508.2—dc22

2010000048

Editor: **Shelly Lyons**
Designer: **Alison Thiele**
Art Director: **Nathan Gassman**
Production Specialist: **Laura Manthe**

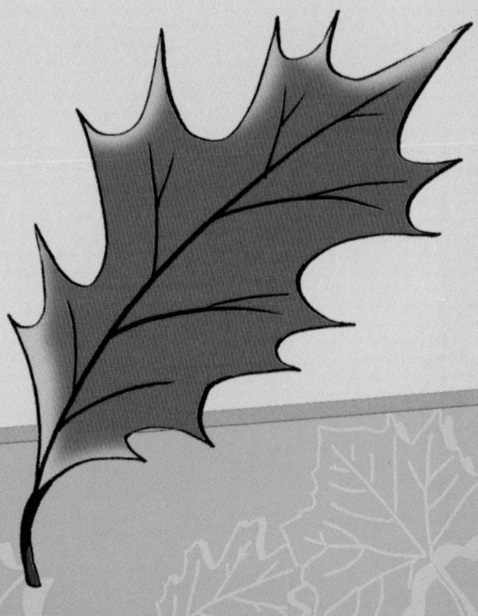

TABLE OF CONTENTS

IT'S FALL!

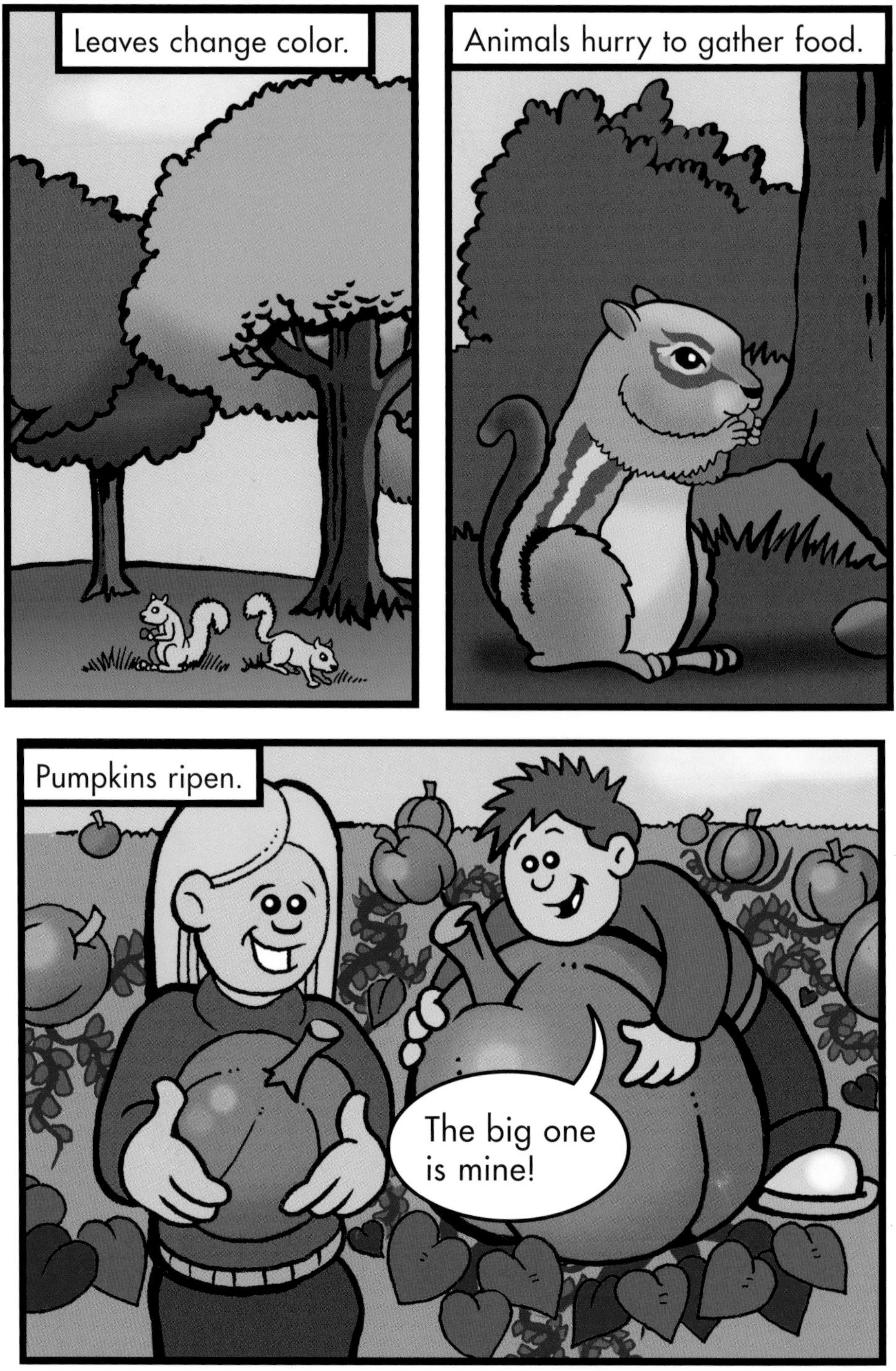
Leaves change color.
Animals hurry to gather food.
Pumpkins ripen.
The big one is mine!

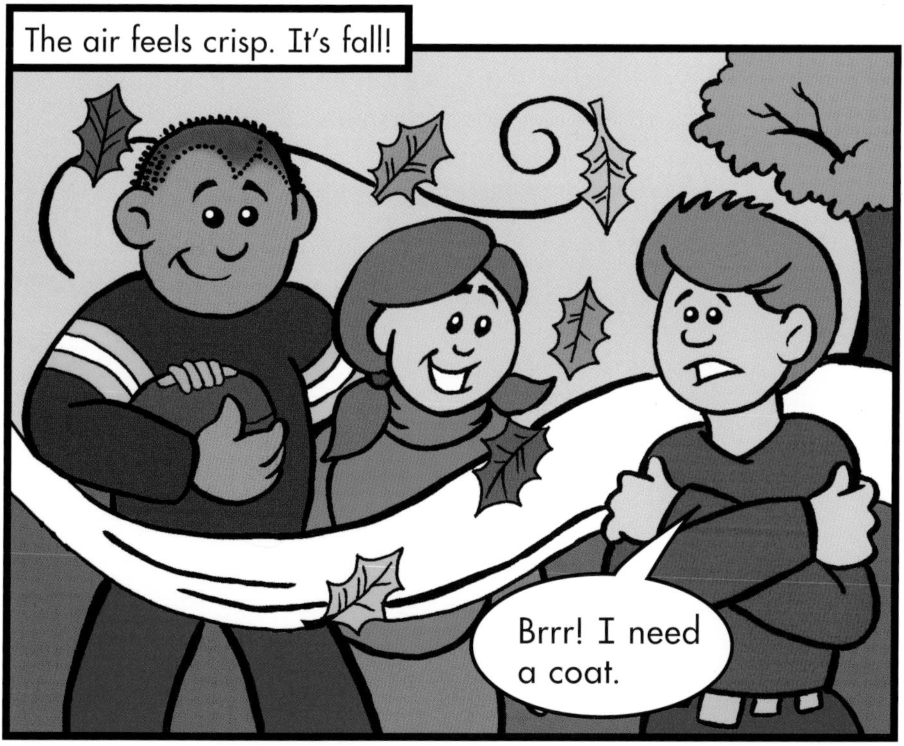
The air feels crisp. It's fall!
Brrr! I need a coat.

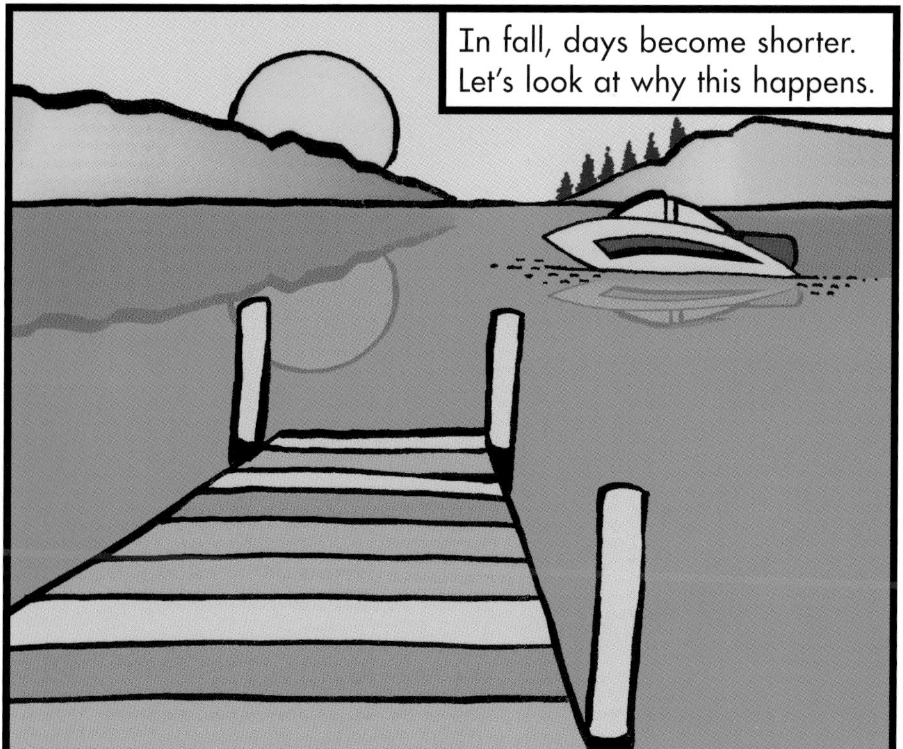
In fall, days become shorter. Let's look at why this happens.

Earth is always tilted at the same angle. It moves around the sun once in a year. As Earth moves, it spins on its axis.

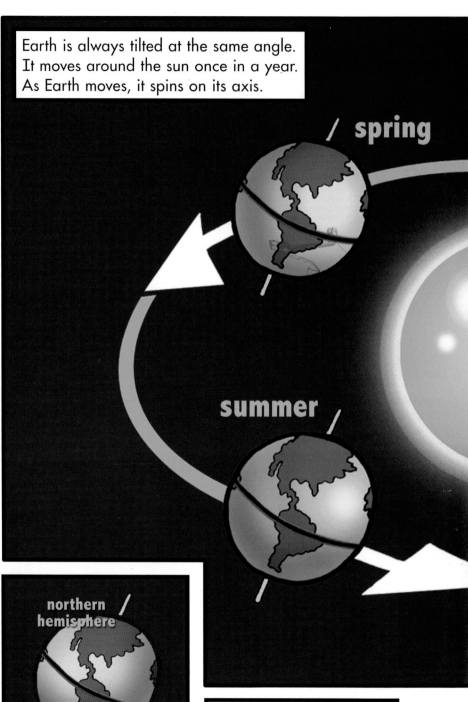

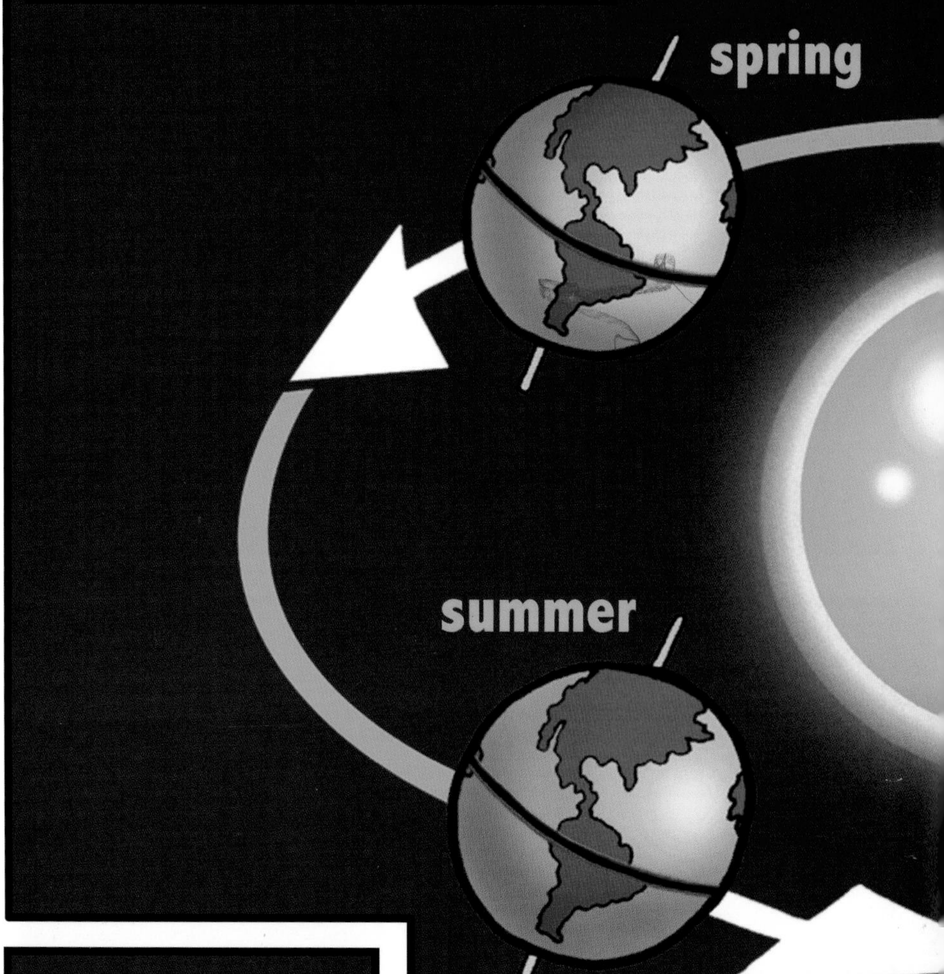
spring
summer

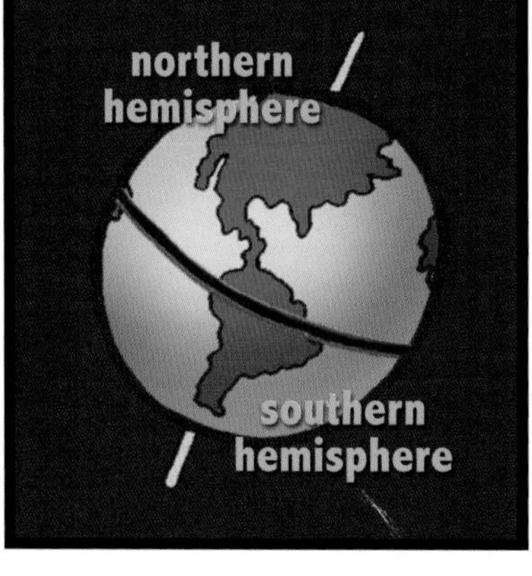
northern hemisphere
southern hemisphere

Earth has a northern and a southern hemisphere.

Northern Hemisphere Seasons

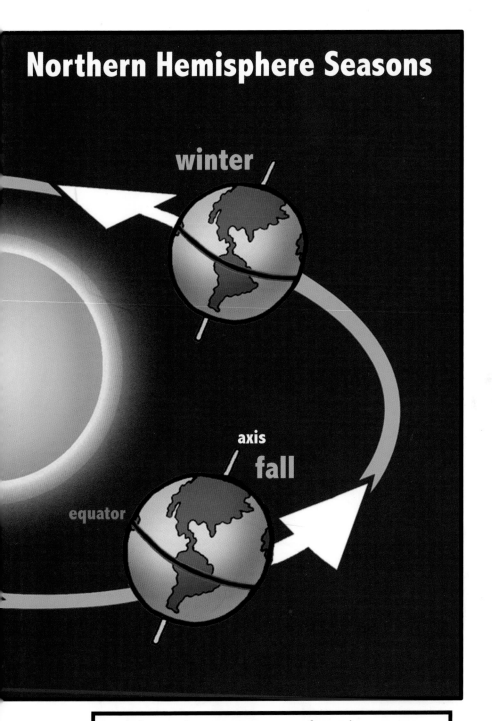

winter

axis

fall

equator

Each hemisphere points away from the sun at opposite times of the year. When starting to point away from the sun, a hemisphere experiences fall.

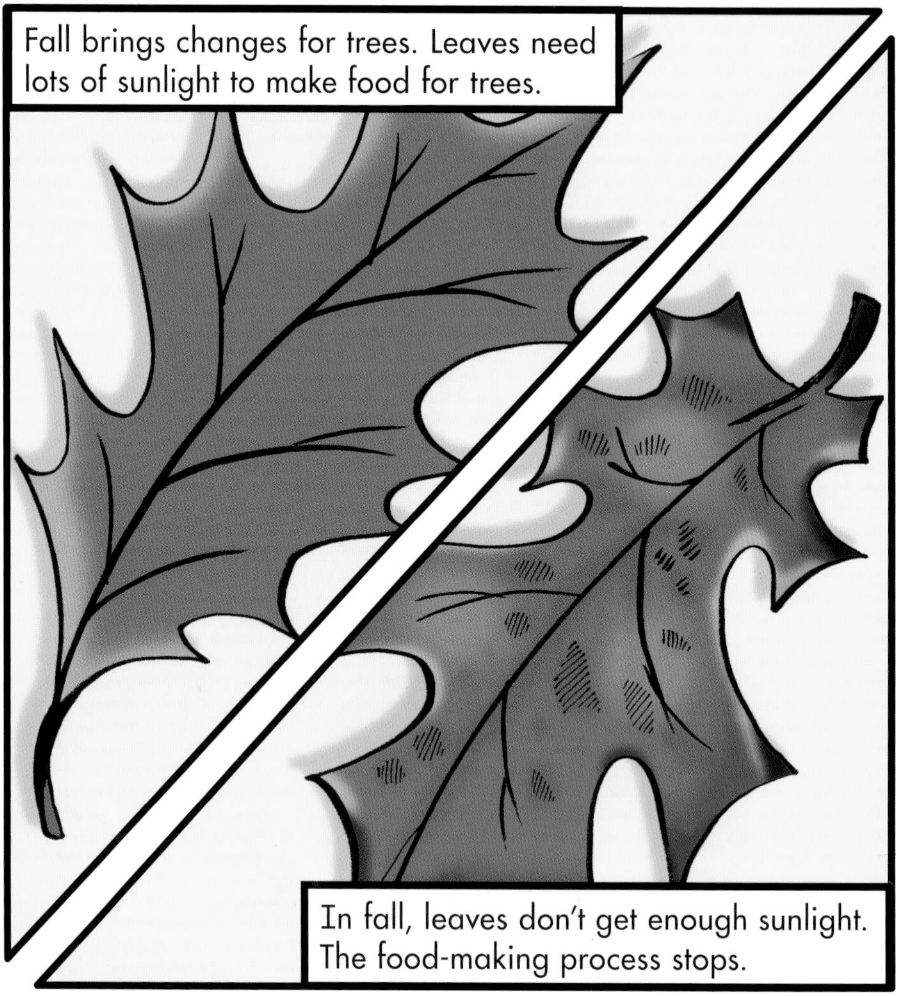
Fall brings changes for trees. Leaves need lots of sunlight to make food for trees.
In fall, leaves don't get enough sunlight. The food-making process stops.

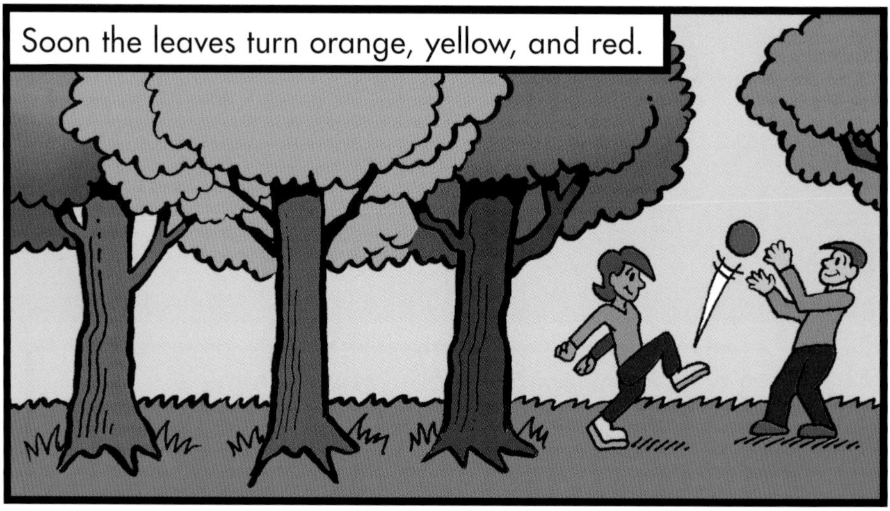
Soon the leaves turn orange, yellow, and red.

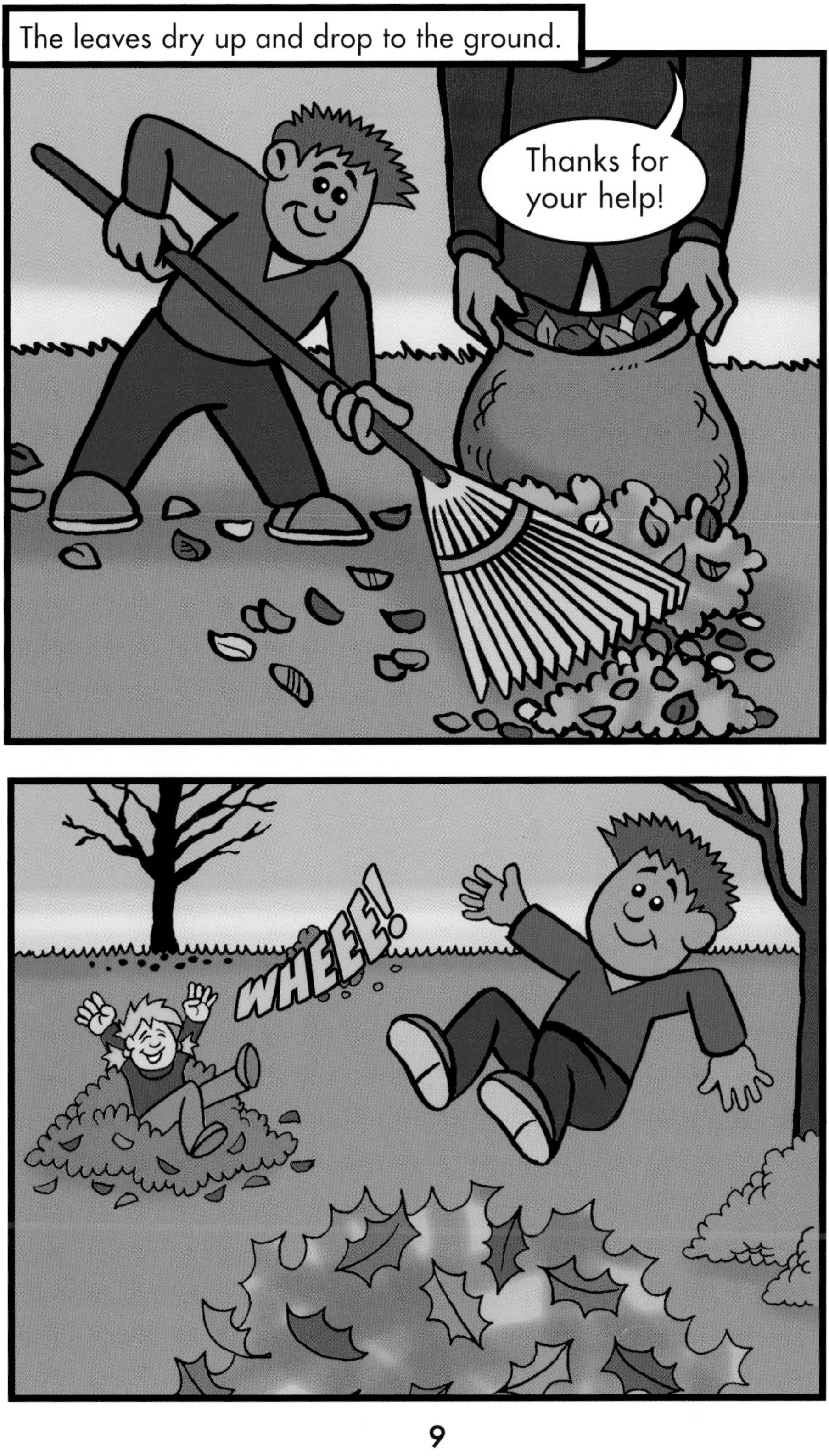
The leaves dry up and drop to the ground.
Thanks for your help!
WHEEE!

Animals in Fall

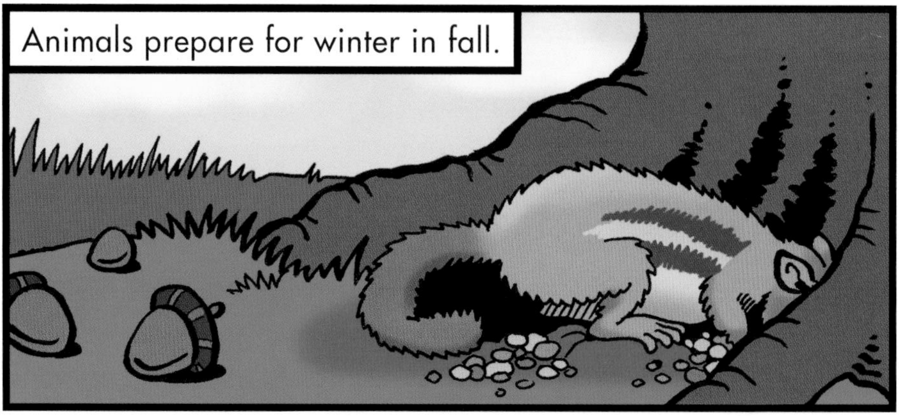
Animals prepare for winter in fall.

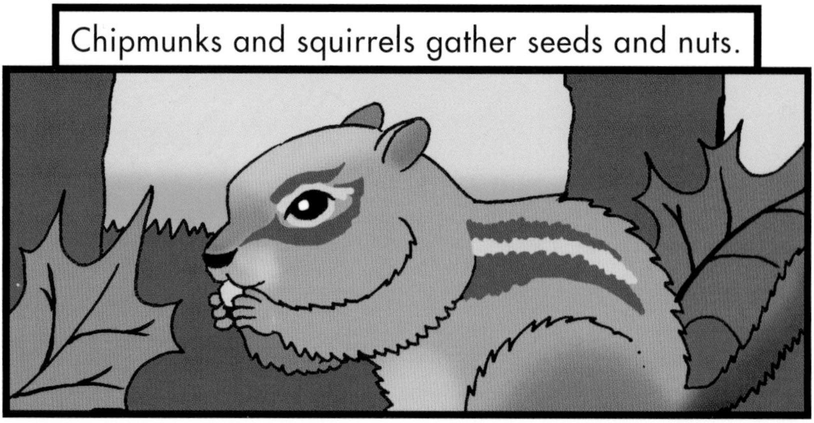
Chipmunks and squirrels gather seeds and nuts.

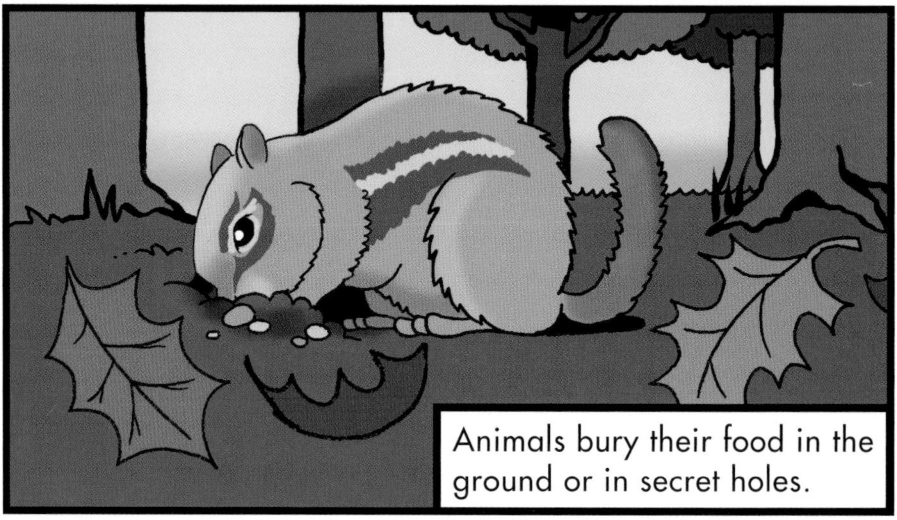
Animals bury their food in the ground or in secret holes.

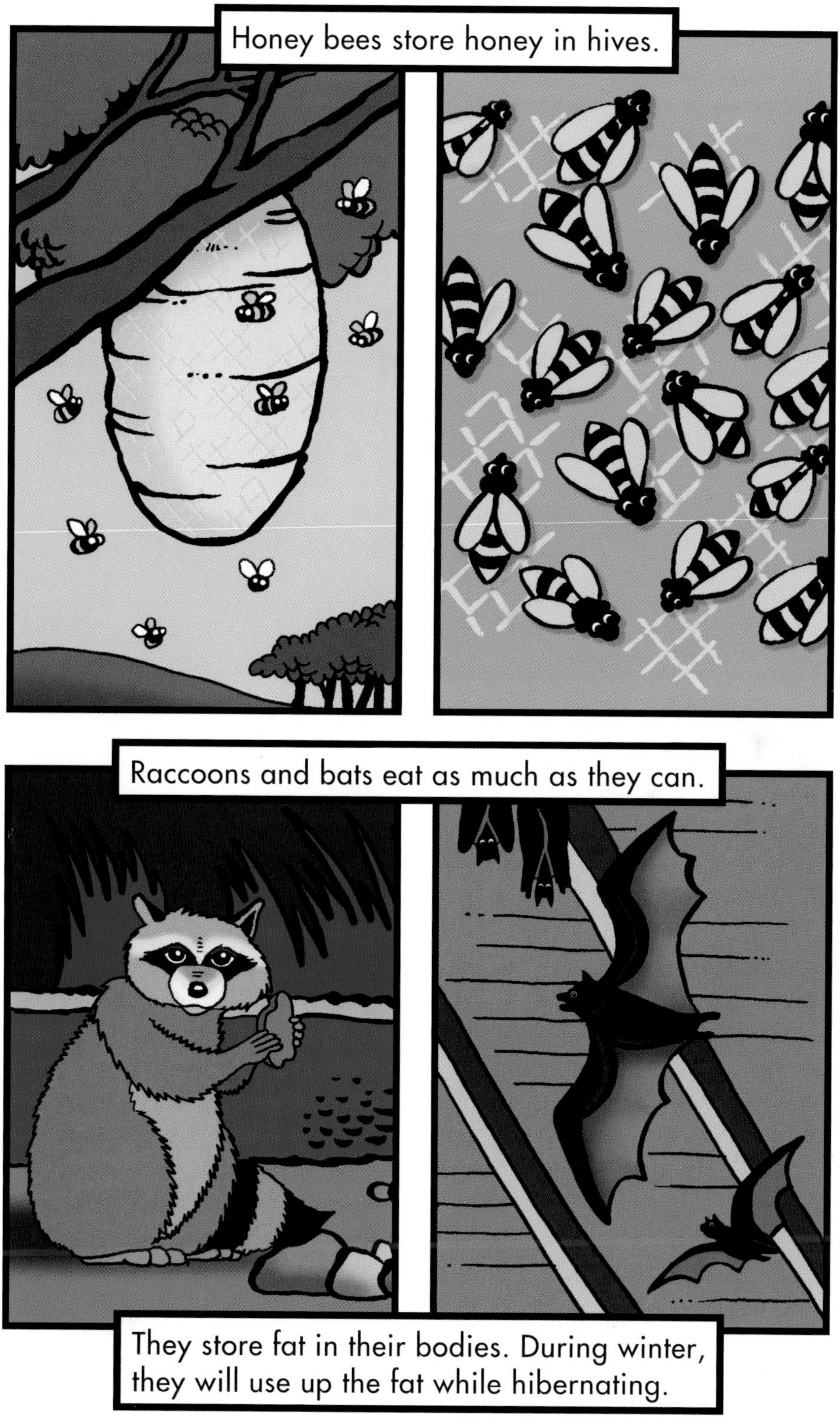
Honey bees store honey in hives.
Raccoons and bats eat as much as they can.
They store fat in their bodies. During winter, they will use up the fat while hibernating.

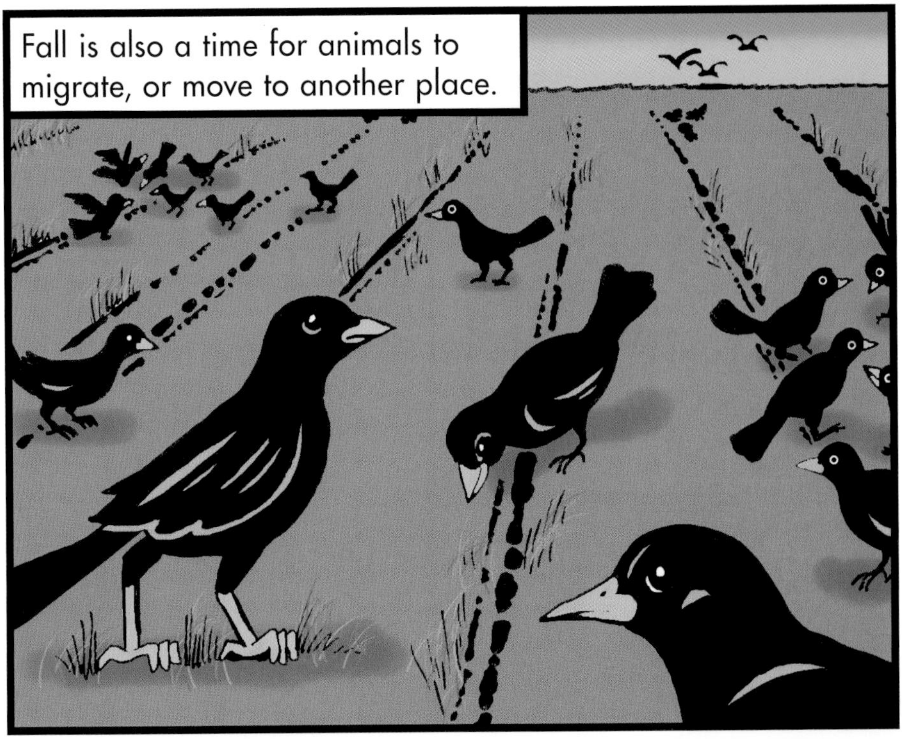
Fall is also a time for animals to migrate, or move to another place.

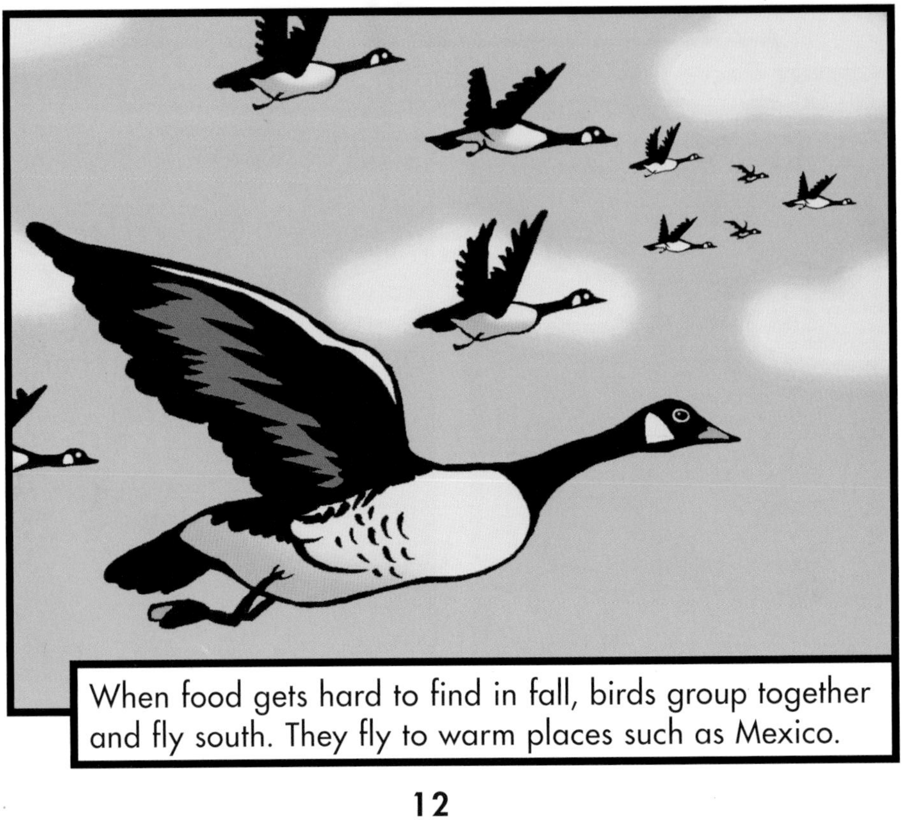
When food gets hard to find in fall, birds group together and fly south. They fly to warm places such as Mexico.

Birds such as ducks, geese, and swallows migrate.

Monarch butterflies also migrate long distances.

Earthworms migrate too. They move from dirt near the ground's surface to areas deep underground.

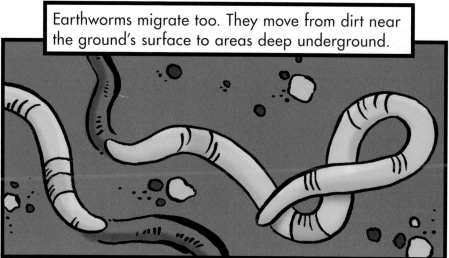

HARVEST TIME

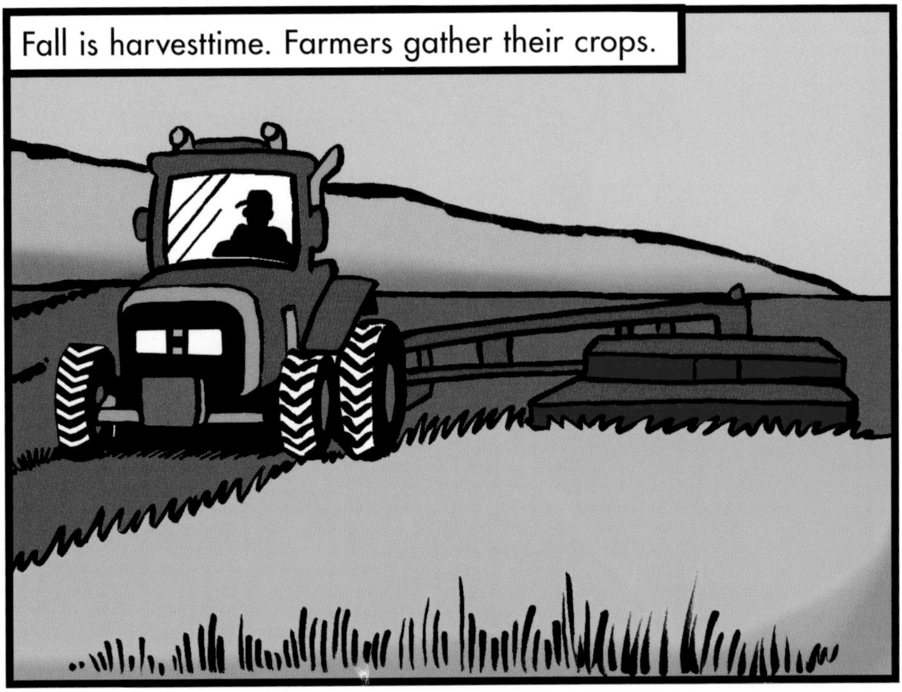
Fall is harvesttime. Farmers gather their crops.

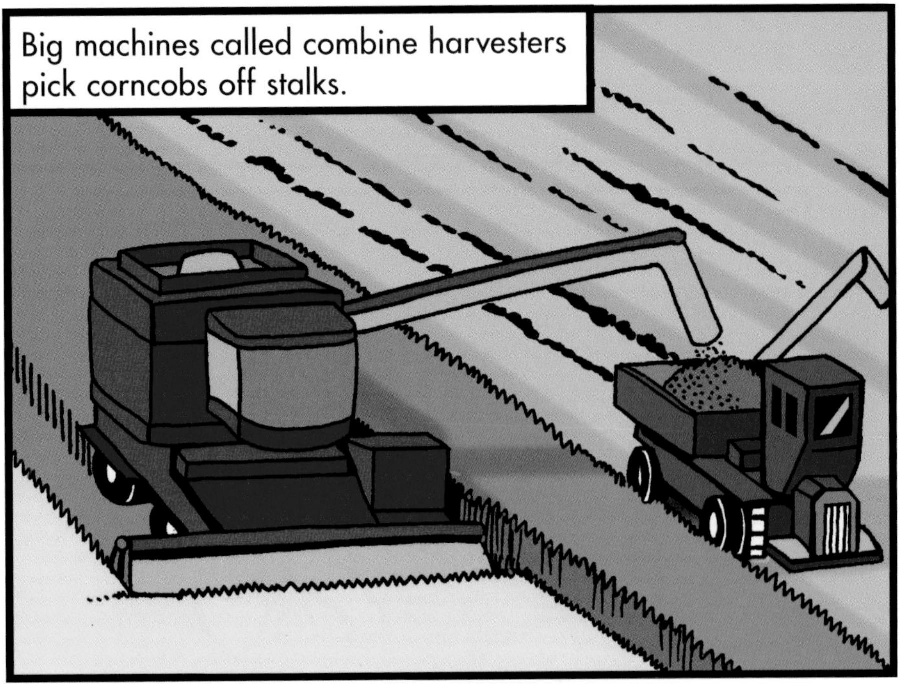
Big machines called combine harvesters pick corncobs off stalks.

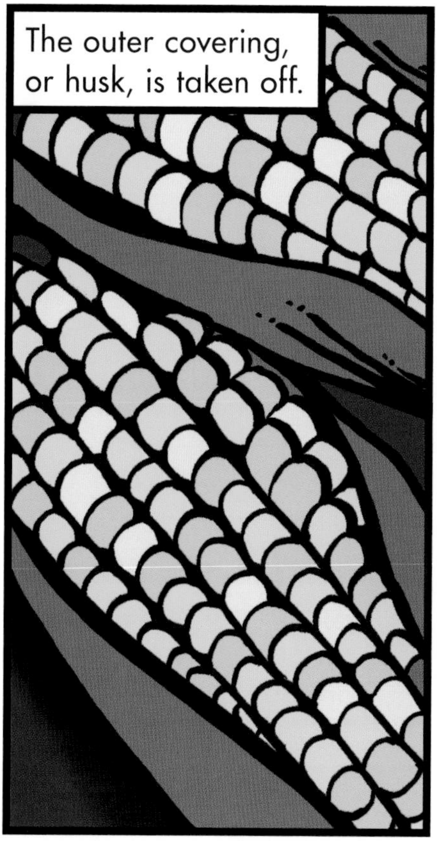
The outer covering, or husk, is taken off.

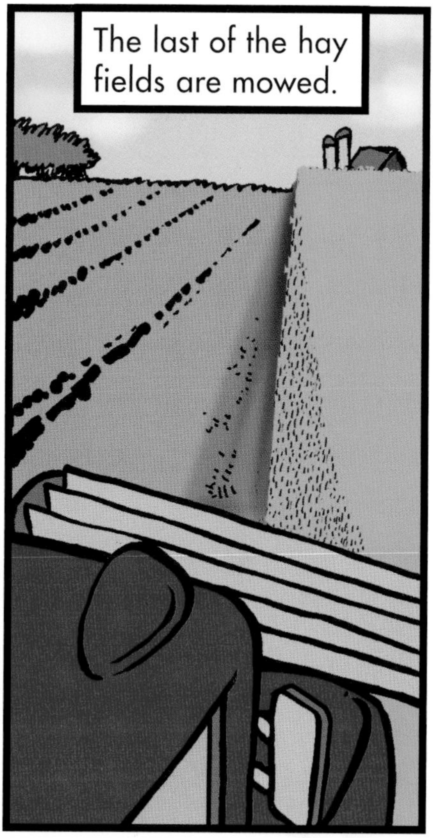
The last of the hay fields are mowed.

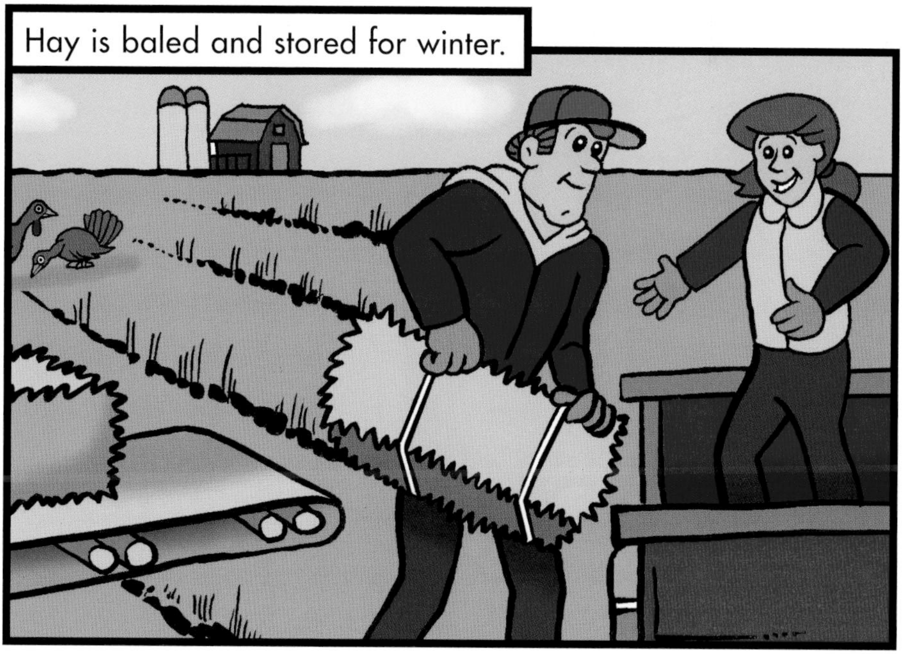
Hay is baled and stored for winter.

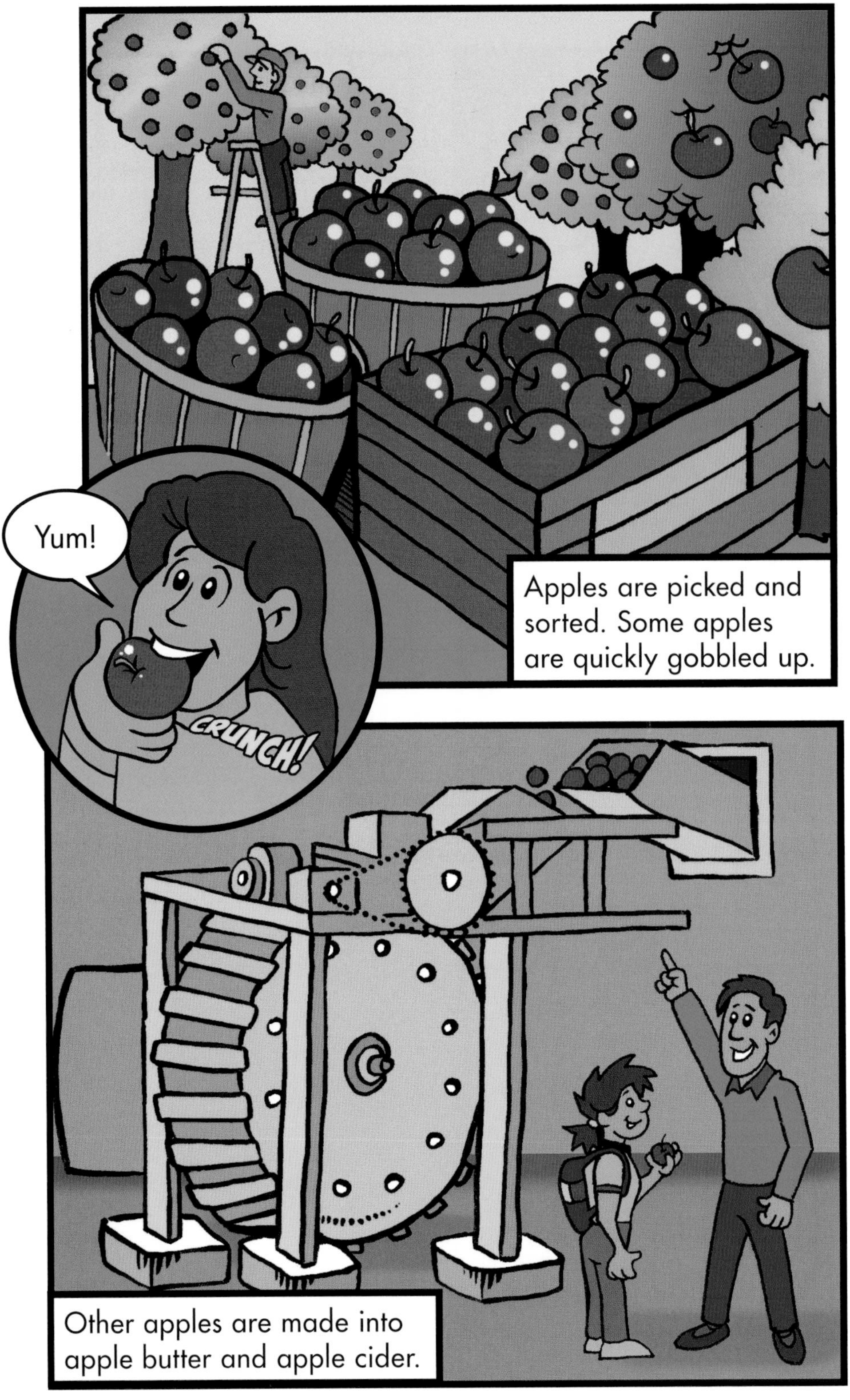
Apples are picked and sorted. Some apples are quickly gobbled up.
Yum!
CRUNCH!
Other apples are made into apple butter and apple cider.

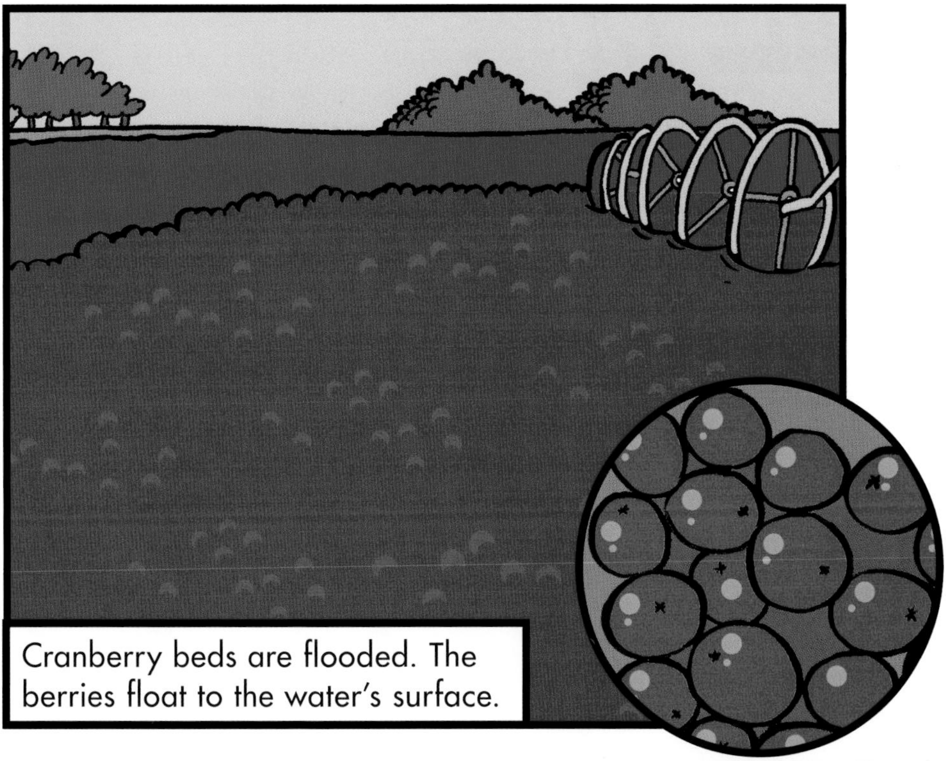
Cranberry beds are flooded. The berries float to the water's surface.

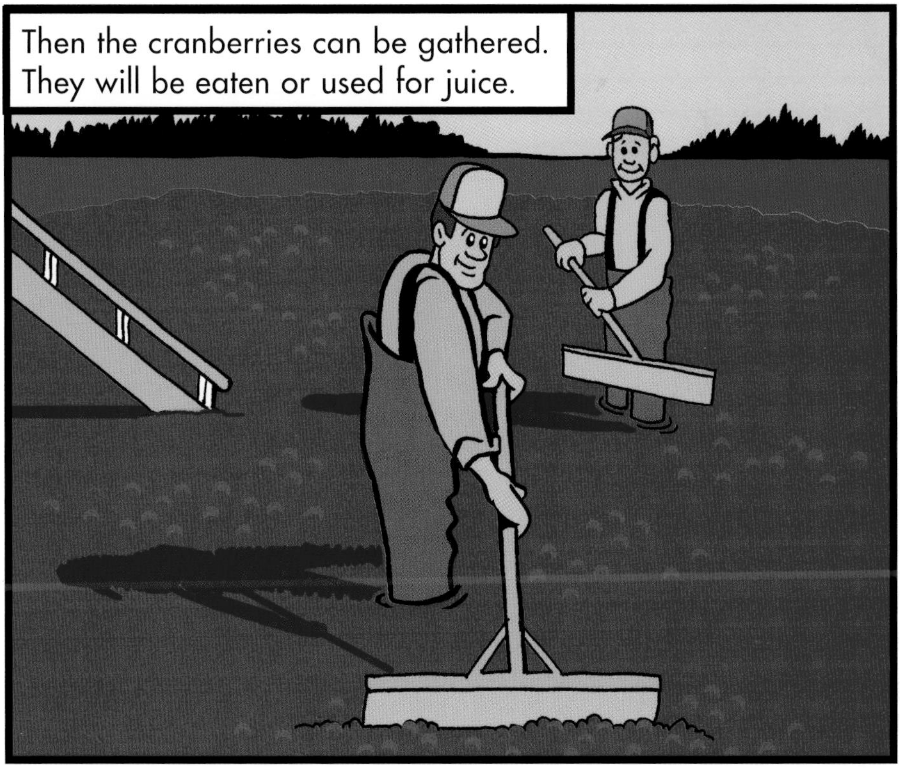
Then the cranberries can be gathered. They will be eaten or used for juice.

Fall Fun

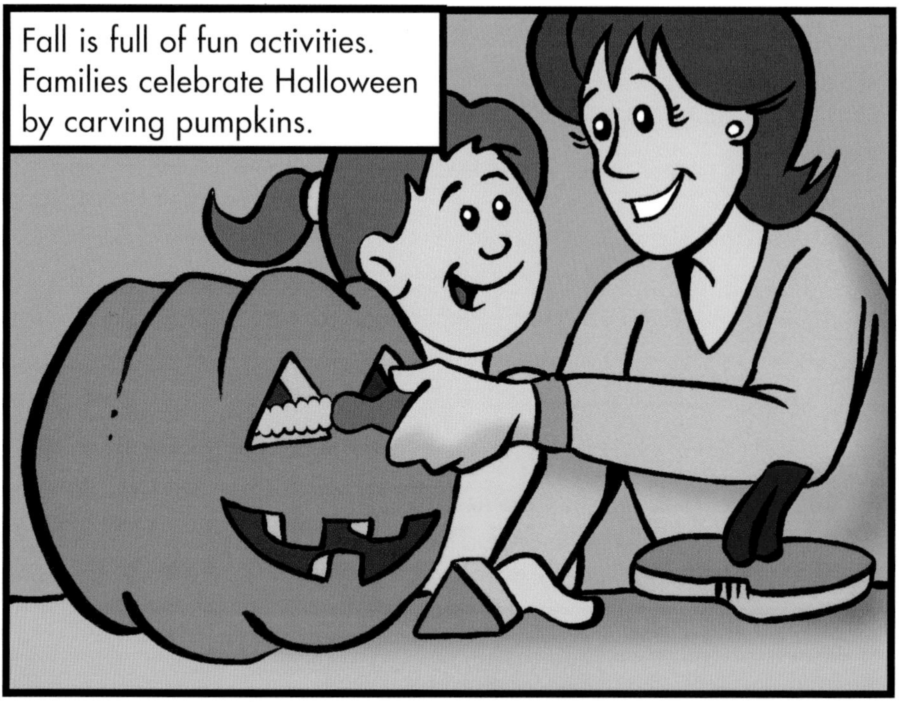
Fall is full of fun activities. Families celebrate Halloween by carving pumpkins.

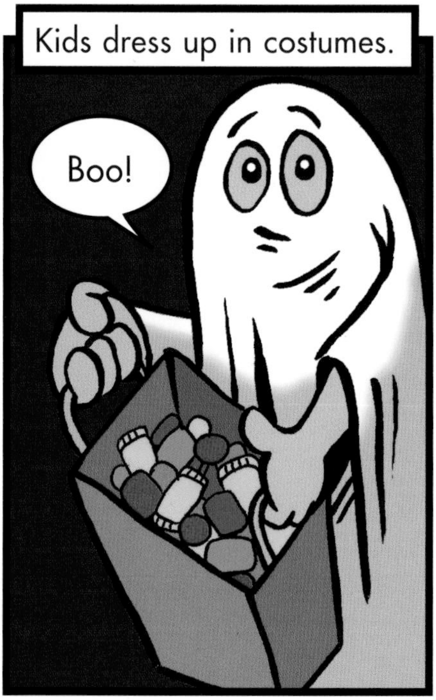
Kids dress up in costumes.
Boo!

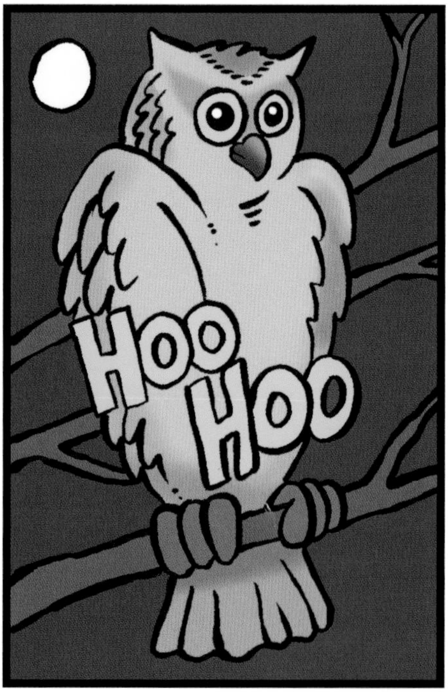
HOO
HOO

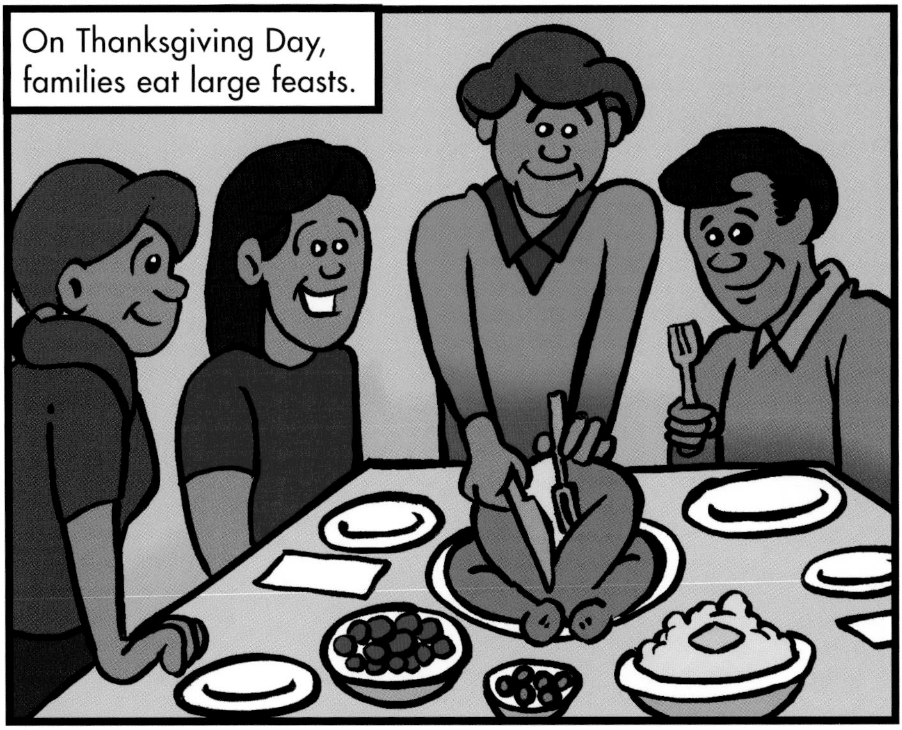
On Thanksgiving Day, families eat large feasts.

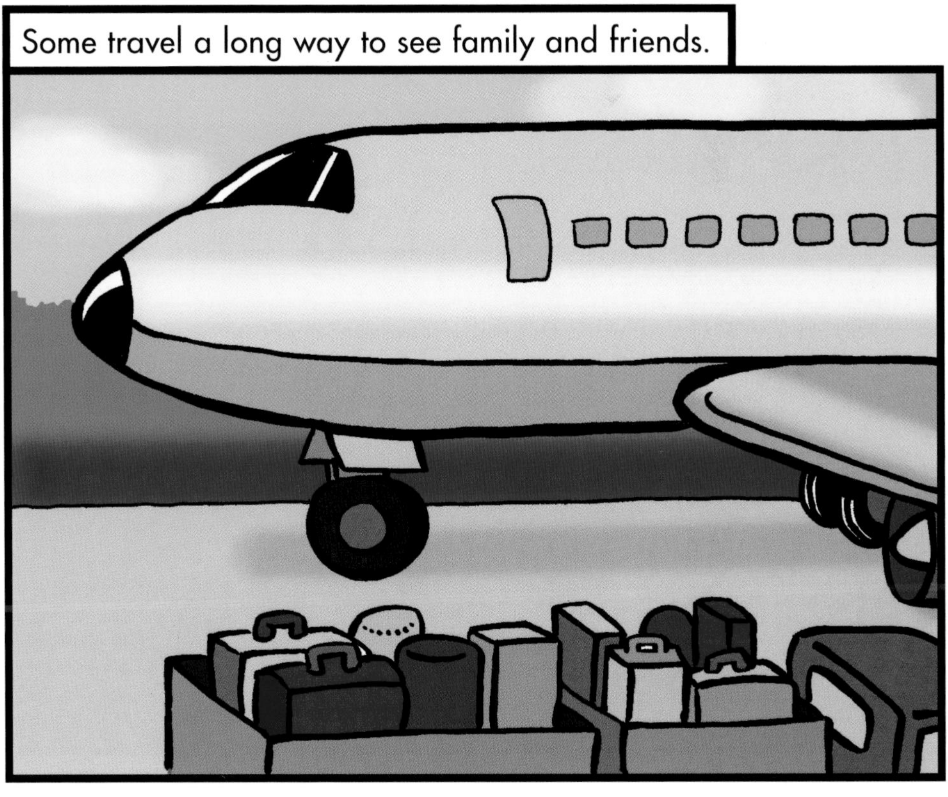
Some travel a long way to see family and friends.

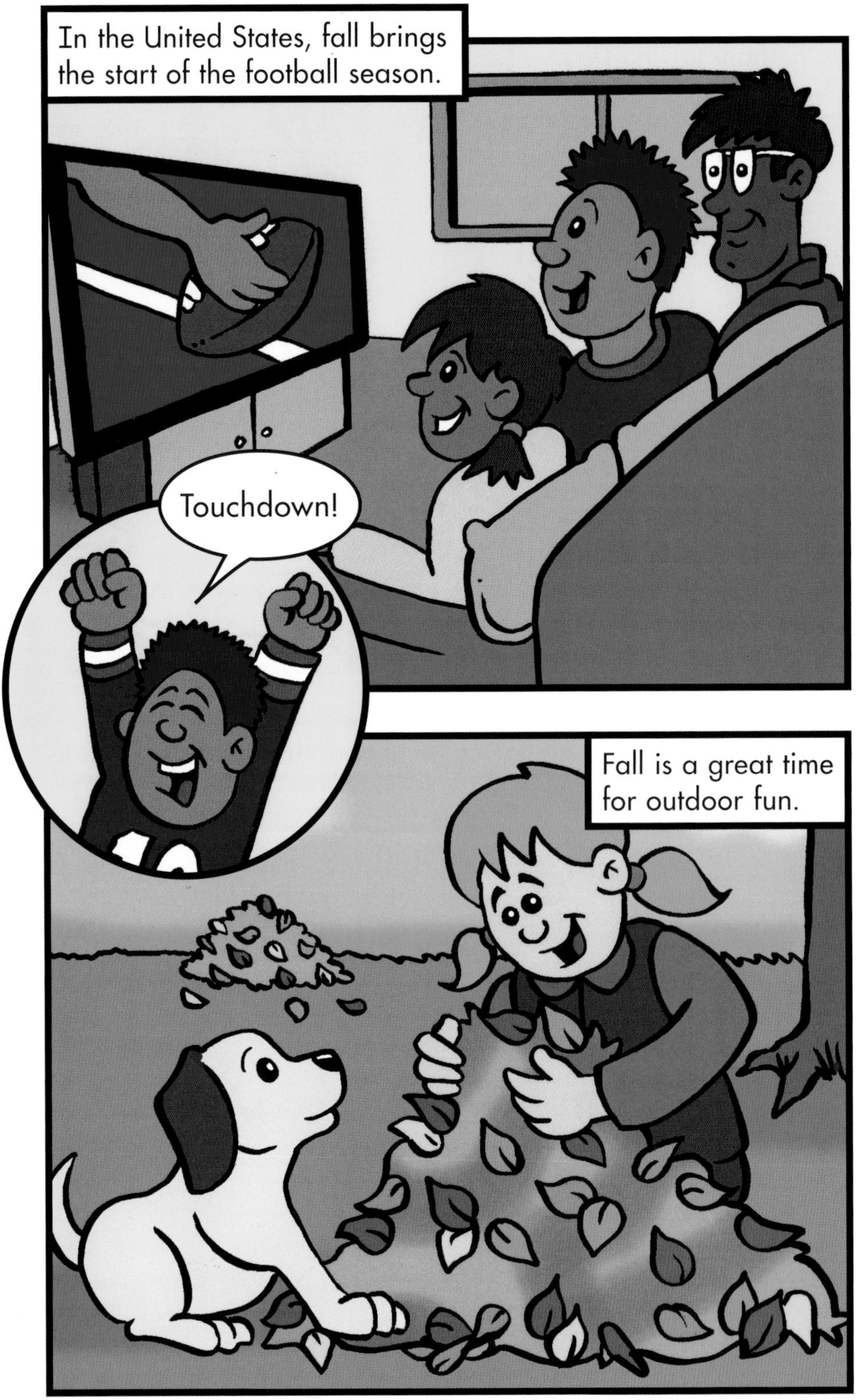
In the United States, fall brings the start of the football season.
Touchdown!
Fall is a great time for outdoor fun.

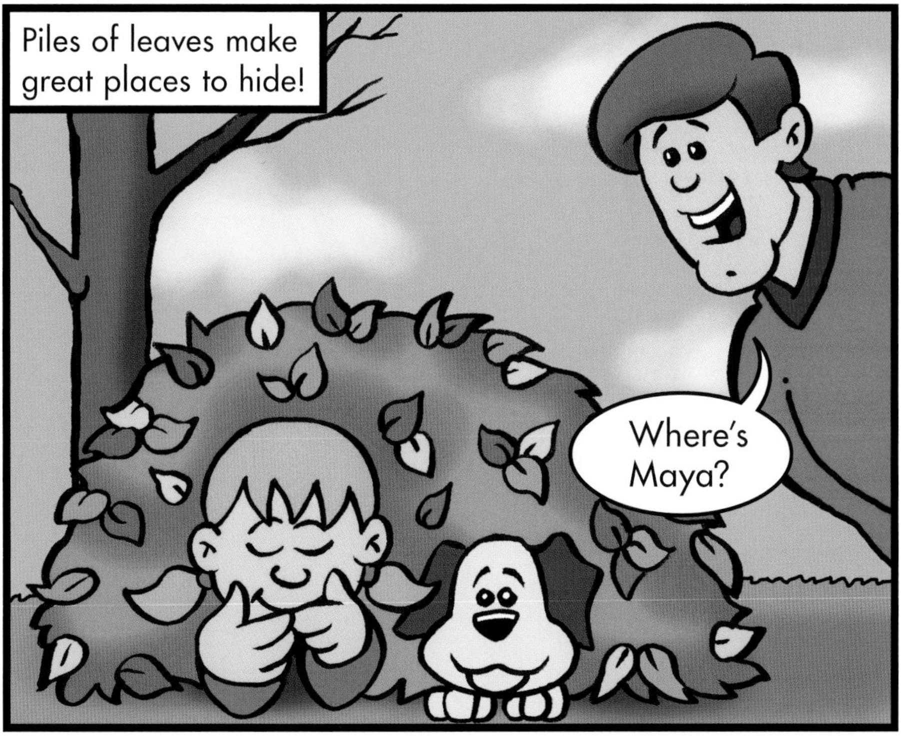
Piles of leaves make great places to hide!
Where's Maya?

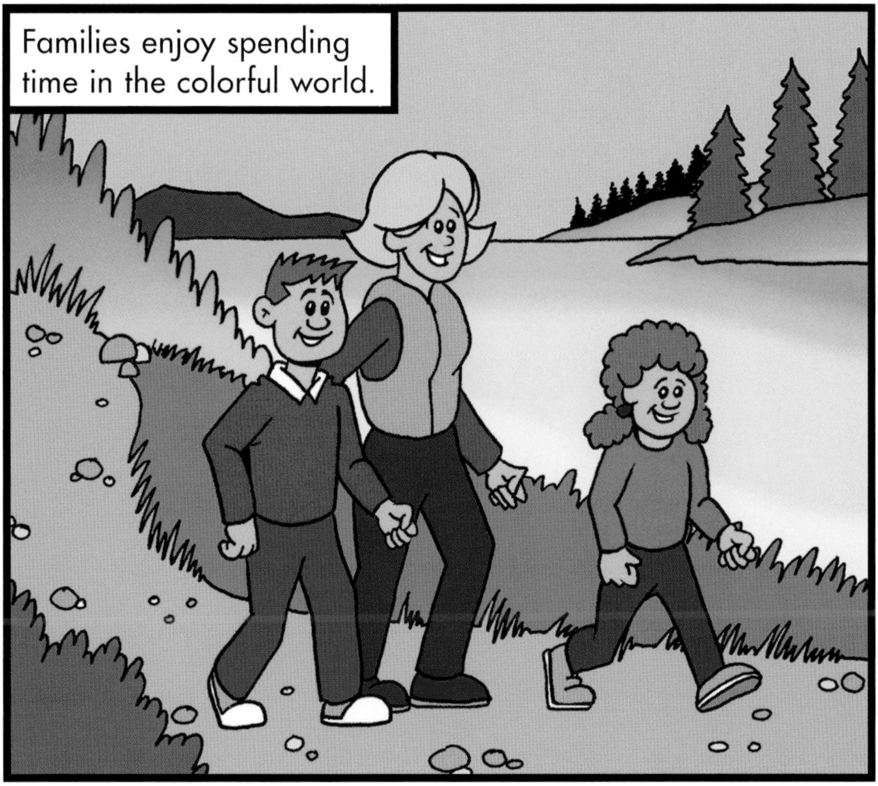
Families enjoy spending time in the colorful world.

GLOSSARY

angle—the figure formed by two lines or flat surfaces that extend from one point or line

axis—an imaginary line that runs through the middle of Earth from the North Pole to the South Pole

bale—to make into a large bundle

combine harvester—a big machine used to gather crops such as corn and grain

equator—an imaginary line around the middle of Earth; areas near the equator are usually warm and wet

hemisphere—one half of Earth

hibernate—to deeply sleep or rest quietly during winter

husk—the outer covering of an ear of corn

migrate—to move from one place to another when seasons change or food is hard to find

ripe—ready to be harvested, picked, or eaten

stalk—the long main part or stem of a plant

READ MORE

Emerson, Carl. *The Autumn Leaf.* Read-It! Readers: Science. Minneapolis: Picture Window Books, 2009.

Royston, Angela. *Looking at Weather and Seasons: How Do They Change?* Looking at Science: How Things Change. Berkeley Heights, N.J.: Enslow Publishers, 2008.

Rustad, Martha E. H. *Animals in Fall.* All About Fall. Mankato, Minn.: Capstone Press, 2008.

INTERNET SITES

FactHound offers a safe, fun way to find Internet sites related to this book. All of the sites on FactHound have been researched by our staff.

Here's all you do:

Visit *www.facthound.com*

Type in this code: 9781429647311

INDEX

SEASONS

TITLES IN THIS SET:

FALL IS FUN

SPRING IS SPECIAL

SUMMER IS SUPER

WINTER IS WONDERFUL